FEAR
No Longer Afraid

JUNE HUNT

ROSE PUBLISHING/ASPIRE PRESS

Carson, California

ROSE PUBLISHING/ASPIRE PRESS

Fear: No Longer Afraid
Copyright © 2013 Hope For The Heart
All rights reserved.
Aspire Press, a division of Rose Publishing, Inc.
17909 Adria Maru Lane
Carson, California 90746 USA
www.aspirepress.com

Register your book at www.aspirepress.com/register
Get inspiration via email, sign up at www.aspirepress.com

The information and solutions offered in this resource are a result of years of Bible study, research, and practical life application. They are intended as guidelines for healthy living and are not a replacement for professional medical advice and counseling. JUNE HUNT and HOPE FOR THE HEART make no warranties, representations, or guarantees regarding any particular result or outcome. Any and all express or implied warranties are disclaimed. Please consult qualified medical, pastoral, and psychological professionals regarding individual conditions and needs. JUNE HUNT and HOPE FOR THE HEART do not advocate that you treat yourself or someone you know and disclaim any and all liability arising directly or indirectly from the information in this resource.

For more information on Hope For The Heart, visit www.hopefortheheart.org or call 1-800-488-HOPE (4673).

Printed by Regent Publishing Services Ltd.
Printed in China, March 2017, 7th printing

CONTENTS

ear friend,

The first time I remember seeing excessive fear, I was a young girl. Our family was visiting a ranch in Wyoming when my brother and I were suddenly startled by screams coming from an adjacent room.

Immediately, we ran into the kitchen to see what was eliciting such shrieks of terror. There we saw our mother and her close friend, Helen, *standing on top of the kitchen table screaming at the top of their lungs.*

What were they so afraid of? A poor, panic-stricken mouse quivering in the corner! (I assure you, that little mouse had far more to fear than did these giant, gargantuan human beings.)

Indeed, there was "a mouse in the house"! But truthfully, Ray and I were so tickled at seeing our mother, for the first time, acting in a way that we considered totally irrational that we—burst into gales of laughter. Their screams combined with our laughter made for a most interesting chorus of contrasts. (It was funny to us, but not to her!)

Most children like to torment their parents—of course, all in the name of fun! And we were no exception. Therefore, when a mousetrap occasionally caught a wee mouse by the tail, my brother and I proceeded to put the live little mouse inside an empty mayonnaise jar. *Then everyone* (especially Mother) could clearly see all of its tiny features.

After poking holes in the lid so the mouse could breathe, we made our surprise presentation. "Mom, we have a gift for you," we declared with mischievous smiles. Mother returned a warm smile. Then as we abruptly presented the trapped mouse with great fanfare, naturally she would squeal. And naturally, we would break into gales of laughter.

For years I've been familiar with the old saying: "Beauty is in the eye of the beholder." How much wiser I would have been if I had figured out that *"Fun is also in the eye of the beholder."* For, indeed, we had fun at our mother's expense. While she was good-natured about our pranks, our presentations could have sent her into a full-blown panic attack!

Now today, if we make the decision to refuse to be fear-based, we need a clear understanding that *"Fear is in the mind of the beholder."* This means that our thinking must be conquered before our fear can be quelled.

Interestingly, God never assumes we will live without fear. In fact, His Word specifically addresses fear by telling us to say, *"When I am afraid, I will put my trust in You"* (Psalm 56:3 NASB). Notice, this verse does not say if, but—*"When I am afraid."* Yes, undeniably there will be times when you and I will be afraid. God knows this to be true.

However, we shouldn't be *consumed* by fear. We shouldn't quiver and quake and quit! Instead, we should simply say to God, *"When I am afraid, I will put my trust in You."* Only then can our hearts truly be at peace.

When you find yourself in fear-producing situations, my prayer is that you will say six times, *"When I am afraid, I will put my trust in You."* If you consistently choose this one simple step, you will slowly see yourself moving from fear to faith.

Yours in the Lord's hope,

June

June Hunt

"Do not conform any longer to the pattern of this world, but be transformed by the renewing of your mind. Then you will be able to test and approve what God's will is—his good, pleasing and perfect will."
(Romans 12:2 NIV)

FEAR
No Longer Afraid

Imagine being terrorized, your life continually threatened, your heart gripped with fear.

Imagine every day waking to the thought: *This day could be my last day—the last for my family—the last for my friends!*

Imagine living in the constant fear of being burglarized and brutalized, vandalized and victimized, mauled and murdered.

Now, all of a sudden, someone appears out of the blue, instructing you to do the unthinkable—*take action and fight those you fear!* But such an idea is impossible—even preposterous—especially for Gideon who is inclined to *flee* in the face of fear.

DEFINITIONS

Now, imagine trying to thresh wheat in a winepress of all places! To thresh—to separate the chaff from the wheat—a gentle breeze in the outdoor air is needed to winnow the chaff. As all is thrown up into the air, both chaff and wheat, the wind blows away the lightweight chaff, and the heavier wheat falls to the ground. But in a winepress the surrounding walls prevent the wind from blowing in the center and threshing is not likely to be effective.

So here you are in hiding, fearing for your life, fighting an uphill battle for a few grains of wheat. At this point, the angel of the Lord appears, saying, *"The LORD is with you, mighty warrior."* He addresses you as what? What's this *mighty warrior*?

Who, you?

Imagine being asked to do something you know you can't do. Like Gideon, rather than attempting to meet the challenge, you find yourself responding, "Thanks—but no thanks. You've got the *wrong* person."

However, the angel announces that you are to lead the battle against your greatest enemy— an enemy that vastly outnumbers your army— one greatly feared by everyone and feared for good reason! The mammoth Midianites have been ravaging and ransacking your people at will, leaving death and destruction in their wake.

How? *"Whenever the Israelites planted their crops, the Midianites [and other enemies] invaded the country. They ... ruined the crops all the way to Gaza and did not spare a living thing for Israel, neither sheep nor cattle nor donkeys"* (Judges 6:3–4). Understandably, your heart is terrorized with fear.

▶ *Fear* is a strong emotional reaction to a perceived imminent danger characterized by a fight, flight, or freeze response.[1]

▶ *Fear* can be real or imagined, rational or irrational, normal or abnormal.

▶ **Fear** acts as a protective reaction, placed in us by our Creator to activate all of our physical defense systems when we face real danger. Fear triggers the release of adrenaline in the body that both prepares and propels us to action often called "fight or flight."

▶ **Fear** is a natural emotion designed by God. However, *fearfulness* is not designed by God, for fearfulness suggests living in a *state of fear*.

▶ **Fear** is a translation of the Hebrew word *yare*, which means "to be afraid, stand in awe or fear." [2] When Gideon was trying to thresh wheat in the winepress and the angel of the Lord appeared to him, *"he was afraid"* (Judges 6:27).

After the heavenly messenger delivers his initial instructions, Gideon quickly questions: "If the Lord is really with us, why has all this evil happened?" And Gideon makes it most clear—if God wants a deliverer, *I am definitely not the man for the job!* After all, he is the *least* in the family belonging to the *weakest* clan in the small tribe of Manasseh. Gideon exclaims, *"How can I save Israel?"* cowering with the angst of anxiety.

Gideon knows that the monstrous Midianites have a new weapon enabling them to make swift, long-range attacks against the Hebrews—rendering them virtually powerless. This terrible weapon is nothing other than *the camel*!

Without food or water and with heavy loads, they cover 300 miles in three or four days. At harvest time, the Midianites simply ascend from the desert and quickly cover the land *"like swarms of locusts."* The Midianite troops and camels, both *"impossible to count,"* strip Israel bare of everything edible. Then, loaded with their plunder, they return to the desert until the next harvest is ripe.

Existing like this for seven years reduces Gideon and all the people to threshing meager amounts of grain in winepresses—hiding food and themselves in mountain dens and caves. No wonder Gideon is fearfully anxious and fully persuaded that *"The LORD has abandoned us and put us into the hand of Midian"* (Judges 6:13). Gideon's continual fear has a "close cousin" called *anxiety.*

▶ *Anxiety* in the psychological/psychiatric world is the "umbrella" word covering varying degrees of worry and fear, ranging from mild to extreme.

▶ *Anxiety* is an uneasiness or distress over a threat or something unknown and is characterized by extreme worry or brooding fear.

▶ *Anxiety* stems from *uncertainty*—hoping something will happen, but having no guarantee that it will … or fearing something will happen, but having no control over whether it will or not.

▶ *Anxiety* can lead to "catastrophic thinking" *overestimating* the likelihood of danger or a negative outcome.

▶ *Anxiety* becomes a "disorder" when it becomes so intense that it dominates a person's thoughts, feelings, and actions, preventing the person from living a normal life.

▶ *Anxiety Disorders*:

- Phobias
- Post-traumatic stress disorder
- Panic disorders
- Obsessive-compulsive disorders
- Acute stress disorder
- Anxiety due to a medical condition
- Substance-induced anxiety
- Generalized anxiety disorder

WHAT IS a Panic Attack?

When the Lord gives Gideon the directive, *"Go in the strength you have and save Israel out of Midian's hand"* (Judges 6:14), He is not giving Gideon a pep talk or a lesson in positive thinking. Rather, He is referring to His own strength operating inside Gideon. This becomes clear with His promise, *"I will be with you, and you will strike down all the Midianites together"* (Judges 6:16).

Nevertheless, Gideon wants proof that both the message and the messenger are truly from God—and he indeed receives it.

Gideon presents an offering of meat and unleavened bread, and the moment the angel touches the offering with his staff, fire flames from the rock, the offering is incinerated, and the angel disappears—vanishes—without a trace! *"When Gideon realized that it was the angel of the LORD, he exclaimed, 'Ah, Sovereign LORD! I have seen the angel of the LORD face to face!'"* (Judges 6:22).

Now Gideon realizes his encounter is with *the* angel of the Lord—meaning he saw a manifestation of the Lord God Himself—not merely an angel. Gideon knew this could mean sudden death! God had told Moses, *"No one may see me and live,"* (meaning seeing God in His essential glory).[3] *"But the LORD said to him, 'Peace! Do not be afraid. You are not going to die'"* (Judges 6:23).

Fortunately, the words of the Lord prevent Gideon from experiencing profound panic. However, many do, in far less dramatic a situation, feel overwhelmed with fright—attacked with fear—and some even tremble with terror. They feel the sense of panic expressed in this Scripture:

> **"Fear and trembling have beset me;**
> **horror has overwhelmed me."**
> **(Psalm 55:5)**

▶ **Panic attacks** are sudden, brief episodes of intense fear with multiple physical symptoms (such as heart palpitations and dizziness) but *without any external threat.*[4]

▶ *Panic attacks* are typically unexpected "out of the blue" experiences. The first time they occur, people are usually involved in normal activities such as walking outside. Suddenly a barrage of frightening sensations strikes them, lasting just a few seconds to a few minutes.[5]

▶ *Panic attacks* can occur again at any time. Sufferers know that just the *fear of having another attack* can trigger one—and so these episodes take on a life of their own.

▶ *Panic attacks* can be considered *fear out of control.*

QUESTION: "Can I do anything to stop a panic attack?"

ANSWER: Yes. When you first begin to experience shallow, rapid breathing, recognize these symptoms as the initiation of *hyperventilation*, which reduces the carbon dioxide in the blood. Such a condition produces classic symptoms of a panic attack: light-headedness, dizziness, tingling of the extremities, palpitations of the heart, feelings of faintness, and respiratory distress. However, let the onset of the rapid breathing serve as a *warning signal.* These symptoms can be stopped by using the following techniques:

► Take slow, deep breaths and hold the air in your lungs for a number of seconds. Then slowly release the air.

► Place the open end of a paper bag around your nose and mouth. Breathe normally into the bag, being sure to breathe in the same air being expelled.

► Place a blanket or sheet totally over your head. Doing so will increase the amount of carbon dioxide being taken into your lungs and ward off the frightening symptoms produced by too little carbon dioxide in your blood.

When experiencing a panic attack, you can feel as if you will die! But that feeling is not based on fact. The truth is: *You will not die.* Whatever your perceived "enemy," claim this truth as you go to war against your panic attacks. The Lord says ...

**"Do not be fainthearted or afraid;
do not be terrified or give way to panic
before them. For the L**ORD** your God
is the one who goes with you to fight
for you against your enemies
to give you victory."
(Deuteronomy 20:3–4)**

Gideon had a very real and legitimate fear that he would die, his fear didn't go away despite God's assurances and call on his life. Following the spectacular experience involving the offering (that the angel of the Lord incinerated), God instructs Gideon to tear down his father's altar to Baal and cut down his Asherah pole—items of pagan worship—and build an altar to Him.

Gideon obeys, but only in the cover of night because *"he was afraid of his family and the men of the town"* (Judges 6:27). Oddly enough, God called this man to defeat an entire army—of well over 100,000—a fearful man afraid of his own family.

And while some people like Gideon experience a profound fear triggered by a particular circumstance—others experience a paralyzing fear without the slightest provocation. This *unwarranted* fear is called a *phobia*.

▶ *Phobias* are persistent, *irrational* fears of an object or a situation—but fears that present no real threat.[6]

▶ *Phobia*, the English word, comes from the Greek word *phobos*, which means "fear,

17

flight or dread."[7] In the New Testament the word for fear is usually *phobos*, which in the Greek language first had the meaning of "flight," and then later it referred to "that which may *cause* flight."[8]

▶ *Phobias* grow out of fear when:[9]

- The fear is clearly *excessive and irrational* (being out of proportion to the actual degree of threat).

- The fear is associated with *avoidance behaviors* (deliberately doing things differently to avoid becoming afraid).

- The fear is associated with *decreased quality of life* (curtailing enjoyment in life).

▶ *Phobic disorders* consist of persistent, *irrational* fears that impair a person's ability to function normally.[10]

- If a phobia causes no major disturbance in a person's lifestyle (such as having an excessive fear of snakes, but rarely ever seeing a snake), it is not considered a disorder.

- However, a *phobic disorder* gains such power in a person's life that it drives that person's thoughts, perceptions, and actions to the point that *the entire life is affected* (such as a fear of darkness or of people).

- Those suffering with a phobic disorder experience the most extreme form of fear.
- Not only are they in a constant state of hyperalertness, but also their fear continuously controls their activities, limits their lives, and drastically diminishes their quality of life.

The one who suffers could easily say ...

> **"Fear and trembling seized me and made all my bones shake."**
> **(Job 4:14)**

WHAT ARE Types of Phobias?[11]

While Gideon's fear does not reach phobic proportions, the "type" of phobia a person experiences is determined by the focus of that person's fear. There are three primary types of phobias—all of which are painfully fear-producing for the sufferer. Typically, those with phobias avoid any thought or sight of the stimulus that triggers a panic attack.

> **"When I think about this, I am terrified; trembling seizes my body."**
> **(Job 21:6)**

▶ **Specific Phobias** (formerly called Simple Phobias) – A fear of a specific object or situation

- This type of phobia is marked by a persistent fear experienced in the presence of or in the anticipated encountering of the object or situation that is feared.

- *Examples of feared objects*: elevators, spiders, knives, snakes, cats, fire, insects
  - *Zoophobia* is fear of animals, characterized by a sense of danger even in the presence of nonthreatening animals.

- *Examples of feared situations*: flying, heights, darkness, driving over bridges or through tunnels
  - *Acrophobia* is fear of heights, characterized by a feeling of extreme insecurity and of falling even when there is no danger of doing so.

  - *Claustrophobia* is fear of closed spaces, characterized by a sense of being smothered in a confined environment.

▶ **Social Phobias** (sometimes called Social Anxiety Disorders) – A fear of embarrassment

- This type of phobia is characterized by a paralyzing fear of appearing stupid or being judged as shameful in a social situation.

- *Examples*: A persistent fear of social situations such as initiating and maintaining a conversation, eating in public, attending a party; also a persistent fear of performance situations such as stage fright and fear of public speaking

▶ **Agoraphobia** (literally, "fear of the marketplace") – A "fear of fear" (when out in open spaces)

- This phobia is a fear of having a panic attack out in a place where escape could be difficult or embarrassing. It comes as a result of repeated panic attacks and is the fear of having another panic attack. Therefore, any situation that could cause a sense of panic is avoided.

- *Example*: Being so afraid of having a panic attack in a public place or in a strange place that a person becomes *homebound* or even *room bound*

These words reflect this paralyzing fear:

"I so feared the crowd and so dreaded the contempt of the clans that I kept silent and would not go outside."
(Job 31:34)

CHARACTERISTICS OF FEARFULNESS

Time and time again, fear resides in Gideon's heart—ready to rear its formidable head.

A vast army has gathered again, ready to raid the land at harvest time. Meanwhile, the Lord has promised Gideon total victory, and *still* he needs divine confirmation concerning his call. *"Gideon said to God, 'If you will save Israel by my hand as you have promised—look, I will place a wool fleece on the threshing floor. If there is dew only on the fleece and all the ground is dry, then I will know that you will save Israel by my hand, as you said'"* (Judges 6:36–37).

God exercises great patience with Gideon's fragile faith, and the next morning His reluctant servant finds a damp fleece and a dry floor. *But wait a minute,* Gideon must have pondered, *might not that have happened naturally?* Of course the floor would dry before the fleece. So he asks God again to participate in another test, but this time to reverse the outcome—with a dry fleece and a damp floor. And *"that night God did so"* (Judges 6:40).

The fear Gideon feels is completely understandable. His enemy is real. His life is in real danger. He has "normal" fear. However, God has proven Himself to be both powerful and trustworthy. It isn't that God doesn't see Gideon's situation or is denying his dilemma—God knows neither is a problem for Him—Gideon needs to know that too! No fear, normal or abnormal, is beyond God's ability to resolve.

Differences between Normal and Abnormal Fear

▶**Normal Fear**

Why would God give us the emotion of fear if it could be detrimental to us? The answer is found in asking another question, "If at this moment you were surprised by an assailant with a knife in his hand, would you want the *benefits* of fear?" Put a check mark (✓) by the symptoms you would experience. Those benefits include …

☐ *Apprehension* (to proceed with caution)

☐ *Breathing increased* (to deliver more oxygen to the body)

- ☐ *Energy increased* (to provide the fuel to take immediate action)

- ☐ *Heart rate increased* (to fuel your muscles with blood)

- ☐ *Hyperalertness* (to increase awareness of danger)

- ☐ *Mind racing* (to provide options to consider)

- ☐ *Muscles contracting* (to prepare for the "fight or flight" reaction)

- ☐ *Perspiration increased* (to cool the body down and prevent overheating)

- ☐ *Pupils dilated* (to increase vision, especially at night)

- ☐ *Senses heightened* (for the purpose of dealing with the feared object)

- ☐ *Sleep lessened* (to provide more "awake" time)

- ☐ *Talking increased* (to aid in communication about the problem)

▶ **Abnormal Fear**[12]

When abnormal fear exists, the level of fear is way out of proportion to the actual situation—in fact, the fear may be totally unrelated to the situation. Abnormal fear can then result in a panic attack. The person with *abnormal* fear can identify with this anguished cry: *"My heart is in anguish within me; the terrors of death assail me. Fear and trembling have beset me; horror has overwhelmed me. I said, 'Oh, that I had the wings of a dove! I would fly away and be at rest—I would flee far away and stay in the desert'"* (Psalm 55:4–7).

A person experiences a panic attack when four or more of the following symptoms occur and reach a peak within ten minutes or less. (The body cannot sustain the "fight or flight" for longer than that time.) Place a check mark (✓) beside symptoms you have experienced.

□ *Chest pain or discomfort* (feeling like you are having a heart attack)

□ *Chills or hot flashes* (feeling like you must get to the hospital)

□ *Choking sensation, difficulty swallowing* (feeling like your throat is closing in on you)

□ *Cold hands, tingling sensation* (feeling like you are going numb)

□ *Detached sensation* (feeling like you are losing touch with reality or yourself)

- ☐ *Dizziness, lightheaded* (feeling like you are going to faint)

- ☐ *Fear of losing control* (feeling like you are going crazy)

- ☐ *Hyperventilating, shortness of breath* (feeling like you are smothering)

- ☐ *Nausea, diarrhea, or abdominal pain and cramping* (feeling like you have a life-threatening disease)

- ☐ *Rapid heart rate, pounding heartbeat* (feeling like your heart is going to jump out of your chest)

- ☐ *Sweating, excessive perspiration* (feeling like you are a huge embarrassment)

- ☐ *Terror of dying* (feeling like you are sure to die)

- ☐ *Trembling or shaking* (feeling like you are doomed)

People with abnormal fear are not as afraid of the object of their fear as they are of the symptoms of their fear.[13] And, indeed, their fear is great. They experience the same feelings that Job had.

"Terrors overwhelm me; my dignity is driven away as by the wind, my safety vanishes like a cloud." (Job 30:15)

Gideon will gradually come to realize that *God's call to a person is never dependent on that person's strength or ability.* God's call is always determined by His own plan and power, and we are asked to respond with faith in His strength. The more Gideon comes to believe that God will give the Midianites into his hands, the more he is able to go forth in complete faith and follow God's plan for the future. Though initially afraid, he moves forward in faith!

Fear can paralyze or mobilize. Gideon could have been paralyzed by doubting God, by fearing that the problems would never change, or by wallowing in his bottom-of-the-rung status of being *"the least in my family."* Negative doubt-filled messages could have played over and over in his mind. If that had been the case, his response to being addressed as a *"mighty warrior"* would have been, *"Mighty warrior?*—not a chance!"

Like Gideon, we all experience times of anxiety, but not all of us experience it in the same way, for the same reason, or to the same degree. Typically, we want to avoid anxiety "like the plague"!

However, anxiety is not to be feared, but to be understood and to be used as a prompt to trust in the Lord all the more.

The Bible advises ...

> **"Do not let your hearts be troubled. Trust in God; trust also in me."**
> **(John 14:1)**

▶ **Moderate anxiety**—normal, fearful concern—can be healthy and helpful.

- It motivates us and leads to increased efficiency.
- It forces us out of our "comfort zone."
- It helps us avoid dangerous situations.
- It can cause us to live dependently on the Lord.

Notice that the psalmist, who put these words to music, turned his focus to the Lord:

"When anxiety was great within me, your consolation brought joy to my soul." (Psalm 94:19)

▶ **Intense anxiety**—abnormal fearful obsession—is more profound and problematic.

- It makes our concentration difficult.
- It causes us to be forgetful.

- It hinders our performance.
- It blocks our communication with others.

Notice that Solomon—called the wisest man on earth—said ...

"Banish anxiety from your heart."
(Ecclesiastes 11:10)

QUESTION: "I have had a number of panic attacks and thought I was going to die. How can I overcome my irrational fear of death?"

ANSWER: You can experience peace—a lasting peace—when you realize that you have absolutely no control over the moment of your death. Based on the Bible, God has already determined the *exact number of your days* on earth. Therefore, face the fact of your death head-on.

Say to the Lord ...

▶"I choose to trust You with Your perfect plan for my life—and my death."

▶"I yield my will to Your will."

▶"Thank You for giving me Your perfect peace."

"All the days ordained for me were written in your book before one of them came to be." (Psalm 139:16)

QUESTION: "How can I overcome my overwhelming fear that my children might die?"

ANSWER: Unquestionably, your children will die. The question that no one can answer with certainty is *when*. That is, no one but God. Realize that God knew and ordained the length of each of your children's lives before they were formed in your womb. This means that your fear is *not beneficial*—it can't change anything because the length of each of our lives has already been established by God.

However, what is beneficial is this:

▶ Praying that you will be Christlike before them

▶ Praying that you will draw them to the Lord by the life you live

A PRAYER OF TRUST

"Lord, thank You
for loving my children.
And thank You that I can trust You
to do what is best for my children.
Since the length of their lives
is already in Your sovereign hands,
I choose to be controlled
by fear no longer.
I choose to trust You and thank You
for every day they are here on earth.
I commit myself to help them
grow in Christlike character.
In Your holy name I pray.
Amen."

"Man's days are determined; you have decreed the number of his months and have set limits he cannot exceed."
(Job 14:5)

CAUSES OF FEAR

What causes Gideon—the man God destines to be one of the greatest leaders in history—to fear the army God promises to defeat? There are two major reasons: Firstly, Gideon lacks military experience, and secondly, he has lived under the oppression of the savage Midianites for seven years. These facts alone are enough to cause Gideon to doubt God's declaration of war against the Midianites.

God's next charge, however, would leave anyone completely paralyzed with fear. Gideon is to go against an army *"thick as locusts"* (Judges 7:12) numbering 135,000 (Judges 8:10). And he is to do this not with an army larger than Midian's, not with a comparable army of the same size, and not even with his present small army of 32,000—just one-fourth their size—but with a drastically reduced and much, much smaller army! And why? The Lord specifically states, so that, *"Israel may not boast against me that her own strength has saved her"* (Judges 7:2).

God gives Gideon an unimaginable directive:
Those who are fearful can return home.
Instantly, 22,000 men are eliminated! While
these men had enough faith to fight, they did
not have enough faith to fight fearlessly—
something God required of Israel when
going into battle. The fundamental principle?
Ultimately, fear contaminates faith. (See
Deuteronomy 20:1–4, 8.)

Now only 10,000 remain in Gideon's ranks.
Then God states what seems absurd: *"still too
many men"* (Judges 7:4)!

Situations that evoke *no fear* in some people
are the same situations that evoke *great
fear* in others. What makes the difference?
Perception! The *perception* of the person
feeling the fear. Notice that Gideon is not
one of the fearful men who return home!
His perception has begun to change! Your
perception of a situation affects both the
degree of your fear (how much fear you will
feel) and the way you will *respond to your fear*
(what you will do because of the fear).

Fear is a natural human reaction to
feeling threatened—either physically or

emotionally—in these three areas: love, significance, and security.[15]

▶ *Your Love from Others Feels Threatened.*

- Primary relationship: "If I lose my marriage partner, I don't know what I will do or how I can go on living."

- Talents and abilities: "If I don't do well enough, I'll lose my friends. Then I'll be all alone."

- Physical attractiveness: "If I start looking older and put on weight, I will lose the affection I need so badly."

- Position in a relationship: "If you spend time with other people, then you don't really love me."

Your Solution: Learn that you are loved by the Lord beyond measure.

"As high as the heavens are above the earth, so great is his love for those who fear him." (Psalm 103:11)

▶ *Your Significance Feels Threatened.*

- Identity: "If I lose my position at work, I will lose all that I have worked to achieve. Then what reason will I have to live?"

- Self-esteem: "If I embarrass myself in front of people, I will never be able to go back there—I'll be too ashamed."

- Reputation: "If anyone finds out about my compulsive habit, I'll lose face with everyone."

- Self-fulfillment: "If I don't complete my goals, my life will be a failure."

Your Solution: Learn that you are so significant that the Lord chose to save you and has planned the future for you.

"God is my salvation; I will trust and not be afraid. The LORD, the LORD, is my strength and my song; he has become my salvation." (Isaiah 12:2)

▶ ***Your Security Feels Threatened.***

- Financial security: "If I don't do well on this presentation, I might lose my job. Then I won't be able to support myself or my family."

- Physical safety: "If I drive too far from home, I might have an accident and even possibly be killed."

- Physical health: "If I am not really careful about what I eat—or even touch—I may get sick. I could literally die!"

- Possessions: "If I lose my home, I will have nowhere to live, and I won't be able to survive."

Your Solution: Learn that your security is in your personal relationship with the Lord.

"In God I trust; I will not be afraid. What can man do to me?" (Psalm 56:11)

Fear does not appear "in a vacuum." Just as Gideon's seven years of terror at the hands of the Midianites set him up to be fearful, something set you up to be controlled by fear, and something serves to trigger that fear. The setup occurred in the past, while the trigger occurs in the present. Finding the truth about your past fearful setup will provide *wisdom* as to why you are being controlled by fear in the present.

"Surely you desire truth in the inner parts; you teach me wisdom in the inmost place." (Psalm 51:6)

▶**Former Fear-Producing Experiences**

- *Traumatic experiences*
  — Childhood sexual abuse or rape

  — Tragic accident

  — Divorce or the death of a loved one or a cherished pet

- *Scare tactics used on you by others*
  - Threats of violence by a parent
  - Threats of violence by siblings
  - Threats of violence by others
- *Underdeveloped sense of self-worth*
  - Neglect, criticism, or ridicule
  - Poor school performance
  - Lack of musical, artistic, or athletic abilities
- *Parents or family members who displayed excessive fear*
  - "My aunt had a panic disorder."
  - "My father was a constant worrier."
  - "My mother was fearful and overprotective."

Realize the reason for your fear and tell yourself the truth about both the past and the present.

"When I was a child, I talked like a child, I thought like a child, I reasoned like a child. When I became a man, I put childish ways behind me." (1 Corinthians 13:11)

▶ Emotional Overload

- *Denial of your own feelings*
  - "I must suppress my pain."
  - "I must deny my disappointments."
  - "I must reject my anger."

- *Excessive need to please people*
  - "I must keep everyone from getting angry."
  - "I must keep everyone happy."
  - "I must have everyone at peace with me."

- *Internalization of stress*
  - "I have a lot of hidden anxiety."
  - "I fail to admit stressful situations."
  - "I have no outlet for venting my emotions."

- *Strict or perfectionist parents or authorities*
  - "I never pleased my parents."
  - "I never was good enough."
  - "I received harsh punishments."

Realize the reason for your fear and let the Lord help you heal from your emotional hurts.

"Humble yourselves, therefore, under God's mighty hand, that he may lift you up in due time. Cast all your anxiety on him because he cares for you." (1 Peter 5:6–7)

▶ Avoidance of Threatening Situations

- *Refusing to face your fears*
  - "I minimize my fearfulness."
  - "I think it will go away in time."
  - "I think that I can avoid fearful situations."

- *Giving no opportunity for change*
  - "I don't seek help or talk to anyone."
  - "I don't try to figure out why I am fearful."
  - "I don't try to learn to confront my fear."

- *Continuing to reinforce your fears*
  - "I accommodate my fears rather than challenge them."
  - "Everything I do is contingent on my fearfulness."
  - "I don't go anywhere that might raise my anxiety level."

- *Reinforcing your negative thought patterns*
  - "Fear dominates all of my decisions."

  - "I evaluate everything through the filter of fear."

  - "My thoughts are dominated by fear."

Realize the reason for your fear and let the Lord help you face your fears.

"I am the LORD, your God, who takes hold of your right hand and says to you, Do not fear; I will help you." (Isaiah 41:13)

▶ **Runaway Imagination**

- *Expecting life to be threatening*
  - "I always expect hostility and hatred."

  - "I always expect resistance and roadblocks."

  - "I always expect danger and disaster."

- *Assuming the worst will happen*
  - "I always assume rejection and ridicule."

  - "I always assume hurt and heartache."

  - "I always assume frustration and failure."

- *Believing you can never change*

  — "I have given up thinking my life will ever be good."

  — "I think I will be controlled by fear forever."

  — "I don't believe God can or will help me."

- *Thinking you have no control over the situation*

  — "I am overwhelmed when I experience fear."

  — "I am powerless when I experience fear."

  — "I can't think clearly when I experience fear."

Realize the reason for your fear and replace the lies you are believing with the truth.

"Whatever is true, whatever is noble, whatever is right, whatever is pure, whatever is lovely, whatever is admirable—if anything is excellent or praiseworthy—think about such things." (Philippians 4:8)

So again, Gideon's troops are thinned! This time God is looking for fearless men who are fervently committed to engaging the enemy in battle, men who will keep pursuing the enemy even when hungry, thirsty, and exhausted.

God has Gideon lead the thirsty men to water where He separates those who kneel to drink from those who lie on their stomachs, lapping water like dogs. The 300 who scoop water into their hands and lap while maintaining vigilance—become God's chosen army to be led by Gideon in defeating the monstrous army of the Midianites.

**"The LORD said to Gideon,
'With the three hundred men that
lapped I will save you and give the
Midianites into your hands.
Let all the other men go,
each to his own place.'"
(Judges 7:7)**

Sometimes people have a physical or medical condition that contributes to their being fearful. There is no indication of a physical cause for Gideon's fear—no coronary condition, no blocked arteries, no heart attack. Rather, God sees something in Gideon's heart that is fatal to faith—a fortress of fear, albeit crumbling, but still standing after living so many years under terror and tyranny. His residing fear is the result of how he has viewed his situation, how he has viewed his insufficiency, and how he has viewed God as having no real commitment in spite of His promises.

Some people, however, experience fear and anxiety when no fearful situation exists, and they become further frustrated when they try to talk themselves out of their anxious feelings—but to no avail. They have no idea their feelings may simply be a reaction to something physical, such as a particular medication or illness.

If you are suffering with a level of anxiety that is interfering with your normal functioning, seriously consider the following steps:

▶ **First, obtain a thorough medical check-up.**

- While you cannot be *genetically* predisposed to panic attacks, you may be *psychologically* predisposed to having them. (Tell the doctor that you feel unusually anxious. Be specific.)

- If you do not get substantial help, get a second opinion from a medical doctor who specializes in anxiety disorders.

"The heart of the discerning acquires knowledge; the ears of the wise seek it out." (Proverbs 18:15)

▶ **Consider your medical condition.**

- Especially to be evaluated are heart, endocrine system, respiratory, metabolic, and neurological conditions. (Identify any deficiency in the B-vitamins, niacin, pyridoxine, calcium, or magnesium.)

- The medical world has a classification called *Anxiety Disorder Due to a General Medical Condition.* This name clearly indicates that a person's poor physical health can contribute to fearful anxiety or even to panic attacks.

▶ **Consider your exposure to substances.**

- A condition known to cause fearful anxiety is called *Substance-Induced Anxiety Disorder.*

- Any exposure to toxins, all drugs, medications, vitamins, and minerals—legal and illegal, over-the-counter and prescription—should be evaluated, along with food substances (for example, caffeine or sugar).

Regardless of your affliction—whatever the suffering—know that your heavenly Father loves you, listens to you, and will help you.

"He has not despised or disdained the suffering of the afflicted one; he has not hidden his face from him but has listened to his cry for help."
(Psalm 22:24)

WHAT ARE Spiritual Causes of Excessive Fear?

Once Gideon hears words of his upcoming victory from the mouth of a Midianite, he is immediately filled with the praises of God and the courage of God. Quickly, in the dark of night, he summons his men and, with trumpets blasting, jars breaking, they shout, *"For the LORD and for Gideon"* (Judges 7:18). Gideon's men surround the enemy camp with a fearsome ring of fire, striking terror into the hearts of the massive Midianite army. They cannot see who they are fighting. Confusion and chaos reign as God causes the vast army to turn their swords on one another. The result is that 120,000 of the mighty enemy lie dead (Judges 8:10) without Gideon's ever even raising a shield or losing a single one of his 300 men—*and God gets all the glory!*

The Lord gives the Midianite camp into Israel's hands. And all the Israelites, along with all of their surrounding enemies, know that only God and God alone could achieve such an awesome feat! Surely the God of Israel is the one true God!

Gideon knows he has to depend on God, not on himself, and not on his army. God is able to use Gideon to gain a great military and spiritual victory because Gideon chooses to put his trust in Him. Because he decides to obey God—in spite of fear—while he is preparing for battle, Gideon is able to obey God without fear in the midst of the battle. He let God be God—the all-powerful One, who goes before us and conquers for His name's sake.

**"Fear God and keep his commandments,
for this is the whole duty of man."
(Ecclesiastes 12:13)**

Gideon's greatest weakness eventually becomes his greatest strength. He discovers that when he acknowledges he is weak and inadequate, God's strength and adequacy prevail in him.

Imagine! God has an encounter with a fear-filled Gideon and reveals truth to him both about the fearsome man of God he will become and the plan God has for him!

Then God supplies him with 32,000 men to accomplish that plan, but gradually reduces that number to only 300 men!

Finally God sends this band of 300 against the army of 135,000—with odds of 450 to 1—so that the *victory would clearly be the Lord's and His alone!* And though no one man could ever defeat 450 men (the ratio God arranged) in his own strength, Gideon *goes forth* with a whole heart! But not until God first removes the final kernel of fear residing in Gideon's heart by sending him among the sleeping Midianites to overhear the interpretation of a dream.

"He [Gideon] and Purah his servant
went down to the outposts of the
camp. ... Gideon arrived just as a man
was telling a friend his dream.
'I had a dream,' he was saying. 'A
round loaf of barley bread came
tumbling into the Midianite camp. It
struck the tent with such force that
the tent overturned and collapsed.' His
friend responded, 'This can be nothing
other than the sword of Gideon. ... God
has given the Midianites and the whole
camp into his hands.' When Gideon
heard the dream and its interpretation,
he worshiped God."
(Judges 7:11, 13–15)

So now, it is time to rally the troops.

"He [Gideon] returned to the camp of
Israel and called out,
'Get up! The LORD has given
the Midianite camp into your hands.'"
(Judges 7:15)

▶ WRONG BELIEF:

"I have no control over my fear. My only recourse is to avoid all fearful situations."

RIGHT BELIEF:

"As I face my fear in the strength of the Lord, fear will not control me. Christ lives in me, and as I focus on His perfect love and His perfect truth, I will feel His perfect peace in the midst of every fear-producing situation."

"There is no fear in love. But perfect love drives out fear, because fear has to do with punishment. The one who fears is not made perfect in love."
(1 John 4:18)

Throughout the Bible God repeats the instruction over and over and over: *"Do not fear. Do not be afraid. Fear not."* God tells us not to fear circumstances, people, things. But we are told, *"Fear the LORD your God, serve him only"* (Deuteronomy 6:13). This fear is not "fright" in the sense that we would be afraid *of* God. The meaning of this kind of fear is *reverence* and *awe for* God. We are to fear Him, be in awe of Him because He is the one and only all-powerful God. He alone has the ability to change us from being fearful of others to being courageously obedient to Him.

> **"Fear God and keep his commandments, for this is the whole duty of man."**
> **(Ecclesiastes 12:13)**

Four Points of God's Plan

The first step in experiencing freedom from the fear in your life is acknowledging that God is worthy of your reverence. The second step is submitting your life and your fears to His authority by receiving His Son, Jesus, as your Savior and Lord.

#1 God's Purpose for You is *Salvation.*

What was God's motive in sending Christ to earth?

To express His love for you by saving you! The Bible says,

"God so loved the world that he gave his one and only Son, that whoever believes in him shall not perish but have eternal life. For God did not send his Son into the world to condemn the world, but to save the world through him." (John 3:16–17)

What was Jesus' purpose in coming to earth?

To forgive your sins, empower you to have victory over sin, and enable you to live a fulfilled life! Jesus said,

"I have come that they may have life, and have it to the full." (John 10:10)

#2 Your Problem is *Sin.*

What exactly is sin?

Sin is living independently of God's standard—knowing what is right, but choosing wrong.

"Anyone, then, who knows the good he ought to do and doesn't do it, sins." (James 4:17)

What is the major consequence of sin?

Spiritual "death," eternal separation from God.

"Your iniquities [sins] have separated you from your God. ... For the wages of sin is death, but the gift of God is eternal life in Christ Jesus our Lord." (Isaiah 59:2; Romans 6:23)

#3 God's Provision for You is the *Savior*.

Can anything remove the penalty for sin?

Yes! Jesus died on the cross to personally pay the penalty for your sins.

"God demonstrates his own love for us in this: While we were still sinners, Christ died for us." (Romans 5:8)

What can keep you from being separated from God?

Belief in (entrusting your life to) Jesus Christ as the only way to God the Father.

"Jesus answered, 'I am the way and the truth and the life. No one comes to the Father except through me.'" (John 14:6)

#4 Your Part is *Surrender.*

Give Christ control of your life—entrusting yourself to Him.

"Jesus said to his disciples, 'If anyone would come after me, he must deny himself and take up his cross [die to your own self-rule] and follow me. For whoever wants to save his life will lose it, but whoever loses his life for me will find it. What good will it be for a man if he gains the whole world, yet forfeits his soul?'" (Matthew 16:24–26)

Place your faith in (rely on) Jesus Christ as your personal Lord and Savior and reject your "good works" as a means of earning God's approval.

"It is by grace you have been saved, through faith—and this not from yourselves, it is the gift of God—not by works, so that no one can boast." (Ephesians 2:8–9)

The moment you choose to receive Jesus as your Lord and Savior—entrusting your life to Him—He comes to live inside you. Then He gives you His power to live the fulfilled life God has planned for you. If you want to be fully forgiven by God and become the person God created you to be, you can tell Him in a simple, heartfelt prayer like this:

PRAYER OF SALVATION

*"Father, I want a real
relationship with You.
I admit that many times I've chosen to
go my own way instead of Your way.
Please forgive me for my sins.
Thank You for sending Your Son
to die on the cross to pay the penalty for
my sins and rising from the dead
to provide new life.
Come into my life to be
my Lord and my Savior.
Instead of being controlled by fear,
I'm giving control of my life
to You to live by faith.
In the holy name of Your Son I pray.
Amen."*

What Can You Expect Now?

By placing your trust in the completed work of Jesus Christ, look at what God says He has just done for you!

**"The Lord himself goes before you
and will be with you; he will never
leave you nor forsake you. Do not
be afraid; do not be discouraged."
(Deuteronomy 31:8)**

STEPS TO SOLUTION

"Get up!" commands Gideon. *"The LORD has given the Midianite camp into your hands."* Obviously, something has changed, something in Gideon! His words could not be more direct, decisive, and divinely inspired. The stronghold of fear in his heart, that formidable fortress of fear, *has finally fallen.*

Dividing his men into three companies, Gideon gives each of them a trumpet for one hand and a jar with only a torch inside for the other. Now, in yet another test of faith God calls Gideon and his men to war *weaponless!* They will face an army of 135,000 with not a sword, not a spear, not a shield in sight!

God asks us to stand in His strength when we're afraid, and that's exactly what Gideon does. *"Watch me,"* Gideon further instructs, *"Follow my lead"* (Judges 7:17).

These are not the words nor the actions of the Gideon first introduced in the winepress. The once cowering man has now become courageous. Clearly he is operating in the strength of another, in the power of Almighty God Himself!

The battalion of 300 men proceeds to encircle the vast Midianite camp in the dark of night and watches Gideon, their leader, like a hawk. *"When I and all who are with me blow our trumpets, then from all around the camp blow yours and shout, 'For the LORD and for Gideon'"* (Judges 7:18).

A bone-chilling blast of trumpets startles the enemy camp. The terrifying smashing of jars expose blazing torches that now encircle the Midianites in a ring of fire. All bedlam breaks loose, absolute chaos consumes the camp.

Of course, the strategic mastermind of this brilliant battle plan was Gideon's Commander-in-Chief—the Lord Himself! Whenever you find yourself in a fearful situation, realize, like Gideon, you are not alone. Rely on the Lord's presence in your life. Focus on His strength in your life. And claim and memorize the promise in this key verse for your life.

KEY VERSE TO MEMORIZE

"Do not fear, for I am with you;
do not be dismayed, for I am your God.
I will strengthen you and help you; I
will uphold you with my righteous right
hand." (Isaiah 41:10)

Key Passage to Read and Reread

In the blackness of night, the Midianites can't see their opponents. Nevertheless, they draw their swords—and attack … and attack … and attack *each other*! Pandemonium runs rampant. But in truth, *"The LORD caused the men throughout the camp to turn on each other with their swords"* (Judges 7:22), unknowingly, brother against brother, friend against friend.

What would you do if you felt terrorized—panic-stricken—but there is no Gideon in hot pursuit, no blaring sound, no crashing noise, just the rapid pounding of your heart?

Gideon learned to rely totally on the Lord. In every real sense, the Lord was his Shepherd—even when he walked through the valley of the shadow of death—Gideon feared no evil because from the beginning, he was told, *"The LORD is with you."*

When you are stricken with fear, take in hand *Psalm 23*. Follow each of the steps presented with each verse. Psalm 23 is the most beloved and most requested passage in the Bible, and for good reason. This Psalm is full of truths we need to focus on in order to have the comfort, restoration, and peace from our relationship with Him.

THE PSALM 23 STRATEGY

"The LORD is my shepherd,
I shall not be in want.
He makes me lie down in green pastures,
he leads me beside quiet waters,
he restores my soul.
He guides me in paths of righteousness
for his name's sake.
Even though I walk through
the valley of the shadow of death,
I will fear no evil, for you are with me;
your rod and your staff, they comfort me.
You prepare a table before me
in the presence of my enemies.
You anoint my head with oil;
my cup overflows.
Surely goodness and love will follow me
all the days of my life, and I will dwell in the
house of the LORD forever."
(Psalm 23)

Certain situations are more fearful than others. Sometimes you only need to read the first few verses once or twice. At other times—especially if you feel a sense of fear out of control—move to an undistracted place and follow each step for each verse. When fear begins to fester, you can exchange panic for peace by focusing on Psalm 23.

▶ *Verse 1:* "*The* LORD *is my shepherd, I shall not be in want.*"

Imagine a grassy, pastoral scene and the Lord there with you. Slowly say 5 times, "The Lord is my Shepherd."

Each time emphasizing a different word:

THE Lord is my Shepherd.

The **LORD** is my Shepherd.

The Lord **IS** my Shepherd.

The Lord is **MY** Shepherd.

The Lord is my **SHEPHERD**.

▶ *Verse 2:* "*He makes me lie down in green pastures, he leads me beside quiet waters.*"

Imagine yourself lying down beside a calm pool of water.

▶ *Verse 3:* "*He restores my soul. He guides me in paths of righteousness for his name's sake.*"

Take several deep breaths and slowly say 5 times, "My Shepherd restores my soul."

Each time emphasizing a different word:

MY Shepherd restores my soul.

My **SHEPHERD** restores my soul.

My Shepherd **RESTORES** my soul.

My Shepherd restores **MY** soul.

My Shepherd restores my **SOUL**.

▶ **Verse 4:** *"Even though I walk through the valley of the shadow of death, I will fear no evil, for you are with me; your rod and your staff, they comfort me."*

Realize that you are not trapped. Slowly say, "I will fear no evil—The Lord is with me." Repeat five times.

▶ **Verse 5:** *"You prepare a table before me in the presence of my enemies. You anoint my head with oil; my cup overflows."*

Repeat 5 times, each time emphasizing a different word:

THE Lord is my Protector.

The **LORD** is my Protector.

The Lord **IS** my Protector.

The Lord is **MY** Protector.

The Lord is my **PROTECTOR**.

▶ **Verse 6:** *"Surely goodness and love will follow me all the days of my life, and I will dwell in the house of the LORD forever."*

Thank the Lord for the way He will use each fearful situation for *good* in your life.

> *"Dear God, I thank You that*
> *You are my Shepherd.*
> *You guide me, You protect me,*
> *and You give me Your peace.*
> *You are the One who restores my soul.*
> *You know my weaknesses*
> *and the times I've caved in to fear.*
> *Now, in my weakness,*
> *I will choose to rely on Your strength.*
> *You are my Shepherd.*
> *I am choosing to rely on Your power*
> *for me to move from fear to faith.*
> *As I turn my fear over to You,*
> *use it for good in my life*
> *to remind me of my continual need for You.*
> *In Your holy name I pray. Amen"*

Focus on your fear, and your panic will increase. Focus on your Shepherd, and your heart will be at peace.

– June Hunt

No knocking of knees, no trembling of hands, Gideon not only leads the charge against the remaining Midianites, in the Lord's strength he boldly stands up to criticism and relentlessly pursues his enemies. Along the way, he and his 300 men keep up the pursuit despite physical exhaustion. After Gideon asks the men in the town of Succoth for sustenance to continue his quest, they scoff at his potential for success and refuse his request.

Sometimes after a great success, we can revert to an old habit—a habit filled with fear and doubt—simply because someone currently in our lives, treats us as we had been painfully treated in the past.

When the men of Succoth scoffed at Gideon, he could have emotionally cratered—even after experiencing such miraculous victory. That is why it's helpful for us to evaluate *why am I really afraid?*

Examining your fear, its origin, its legitimacy, and its pattern can help you understand your fear and develop a strategy to resolve it. First, go before God, who is the Source of wisdom, and pray this prayer from your heart:

"Search me, O God, and know my heart; test me and know my anxious thoughts. See if there is any offensive way in me, and lead me in the way everlasting." (Psalm 139:23–24)

Identify your specific fear: *Of what are you truly afraid?* Then ask yourself:

- Is my fear tied to recent events or did it originate from a specific situation in the past?

- Is my fear of the object or situation a true threat or merely a perceived threat?

- Is my fear wrongly associated with an event or object that should not be feared?

- Is my fear coming from certain places, people, or things that remind me of possible fearful consequences?

- Is my fear due to a persistent fear-based mentality—even though the relationship or lifestyle in which it was rooted no longer exists?

- Is my fear a result of having faked fear to get attention over such a long period of time that the fear has now become real to me?

"The wisdom of the prudent is to give thought to their ways, but the folly of fools is deception." (Proverbs 14:8)

Gideon makes the same request for supplies at a second town—Peniel—and receives the same refusal. In resuming his pursuit of the Midianite kings, Gideon and his men rout the entire remaining army of 15,000 and capture their cruel kings. Gideon continues living out his personal transformation from fear to faith as he completes the task God has called him to accomplish: delivering Israel from the destructive domination of the Midianites. And he does it in the face of criticism and opposition, not only from his enemies, but from his countrymen. And he does it because he knows that his God, his source for truth, is trustworthy.

Knowing the truth and then acting on the truth is critical to conquering fear. The source of truth is the One who does not lie—our God who *cannot* lie.

The first step in applying truth is to identify the false assumptions behind the fears you are experiencing and to replace the false with the truth.

"You will know the truth, and the truth will set you free." (John 8:32)

When you feel afraid of a person or a situation ...

▶ *Ask yourself if what you are afraid of is certain to happen.*

- Evaluate: "Is what I fear actually likely to happen?"

- Realize that fixating on your fear guarantees its repetition.

- Understand that most fears have nothing to do with what's happening now.

▶ *Determine how current the fear that you are presently feeling is. Ask yourself ...*

- What was the past trauma(s) that first instigated my fear?

- What past fear am I bringing into the present?

- When did this fear first begin?

- How old am I emotionally when I am feeling this fear?

- Where am I when I am feeling this fear?

- What is going on when I am feeling this fear?

- How is this fear affecting my life now? What is it costing me?

▶ *Decide: Are you determined to get out of the grip of fear? If so …*

- Do what it takes to control your fear and to change from being fearful. Tell yourself, "I will not let this fear run my life. … I will not let past fears control me."

- Decide to live in the here and now and act in a way that is not based on fear. Repeat this phrase over and over, "That was then, and this is now. That was then, and this is now."

- Share your fear and your plan for change with a trustworthy person.

As you choose to face your fear with faith, claim this Scripture as your own:

"I sought the Lord,
and he answered me;
he delivered me from all my fears."
(Psalm 34:4)

Gideon moves from the testing of God to triumph with God from a fear-based fleece to a faith-based foundation. Previously, Gideon kept asking God for supernatural signs affirming that God would do what He clearly and repeatedly said He would do. (See Judges 6:36–40.)

Ultimately, Gideon moves from weakness to strength, from doubt to faith, from vacillating to victorious—and he does so by trusting in the one true God and taking action based on that trust. For it is God who gives Gideon victories in defeating both his foes and his fears.

Because of Gideon's successes in saving his people from perishing, in conquering enemy kings, and in gaining victory over vast armies, his people ask him to rule over them. However, Gideon tells them, *"I will not rule over you. … The LORD will rule over you"* (Judges 8:23).

God's call on Gideon's life is clear: he is to go in the Lord's strength and *"save Israel out of Midian's hand"* (Judges 6:14). But that call does not include *ruling* over Israel. Gideon knows this, and he also knows that God is not to be replaced by the man He made into a *"mighty warrior*" and empowered to accomplish His purposes. Gideon is still just a man and God is still the Almighty Ruler of the universe.

As you seek to follow Gideon's example in moving from fear to faith …

▶ *Begin with a healthy fear (awe) of God.*

- Believe that God created you because He loves you.
- Believe that God has a purpose and a plan for your life.
- Believe that God has the right to have authority over you.
- Believe that God wants you to entrust your life to Him.
- Believe that God has the power to change you.
- Believe that God will keep you safe as you trust in Him.

"*The fear of the LORD is the beginning of knowledge, but fools despise wisdom and discipline.*" (Proverbs 1:7)

▶ *Be aware that living in a "state of fear" is not part of God's plan for you.*

- Fear-based thinking suggests you may not be fully trusting God.
- Fear-based thinking does not appropriate the grace of God.

- Fear-based thinking keeps you in bondage to fear.

- Fear-based thinking is physically, emotionally, and spiritually damaging.

"In God I trust; I will not be afraid. What can mortal man do to me?" (Psalm 56:4)

▶ ***Be willing to analyze your fear honestly to discover the real source of your fear.***

- Fear of rejection. Do you need to be loved?

- Fear of failure. Do you need to feel significant?

- Fear of financial loss. Do you need to feel secure?

"Fear of man will prove to be a snare, but whoever trusts in the LORD is kept safe." (Proverbs 29:25)

▶ ***Be aware of the power of God's love for you.***

- God's love provides you with complete acceptance.

- God's love provides you with a realization of your true value.

- God's love provides you with the power to overcome fear.

- God's love provides you with true security.

"I have loved you with an everlasting love; I have drawn you with loving-kindness." (Jeremiah 31:3)

▶ *Be committed to developing your faith in the Lord.*

- Be actively involved in a Bible study. (2 Timothy 2:15)

- Be in daily prayer—truly talking with God. (Philippians 4:6)

- Be consistently active in a local church that teaches the Word of God. (Hebrews 10:25)

- Be committed to memorizing and meditating on God's Word. (Philippians 4:8)

- Be obedient to God's promptings in your spirit. (Philippians 4:5)

"His delight is in the law of the LORD, and on his law he meditates day and night." (Psalm 1:2)

▶ *Be involved with other believers.*

- Be engaged with fellow Christians. (Hebrews 10:25)

- Be willing to testify to God's faithfulness in your life. (Lamentations 3:22–23)

- Be focused on serving others. (Philippians 4:10)

- Be aware of the twofold responsibility (Christ's and yours) in assisting others in need. (Philippians 4:13–14)

- Be accountable to a small intimate group of growing Christians.

"As iron sharpens iron, so one man sharpens another." (Proverbs 27:17)

▶ ***Begin using truth from God's Word*** to rein in your fear-producing imagination the moment it starts spinning out of control.

- *"When I am afraid, I will trust in you."* (Psalm 56:3)

- *"The LORD is my light and my salvation—whom shall I fear? The LORD is the stronghold of my life—of whom shall I be afraid?"* (Psalm 27:1)

- *"God is our refuge and strength, an ever-present help in trouble."* (Psalm 46:1)

▶ ***Be willing to face the situations*** you fear through faith in the power of Christ.

- Know that Christ is always ready to respond to your needs.

- Acknowledge His actual presence and call for His help.

- Release your fear to Him and receive His powerful love.

- Act in love toward others by focusing on their needs and relying on God.

"The one who calls you is faithful and he will do it." (1 Thessalonians 5:24)

▶ ***Become free*** from your fear and strengthened in your faith.

- Become more trusting.
- Become more peaceful.
- Become more thankful.
- Become more Christlike.

"Just as you received Christ Jesus as Lord, continue to live in him, rooted and built up in him, strengthened in the faith as you were taught, and overflowing with thankfulness." (Colossians 2:6–7)

HOW TO Decrease Your Fear with "Desensitization"[17]

In spite of his enormous initial fear, Gideon eventually accomplishes the supernatural in the power of God because he believes in the promises of God and acts on them in faith. At first, he sees himself as a weak thresher, but God sees him as a *"mighty warrior."* Then, as Gideon takes God at His word and acts out of faith rather than out of fear, his faith in God grows, his courage as a warrior grows, and finally he comes to see himself as God sees him. With each progressively more fearful situation, God's reassurance helps Gideon to choose, as an act of his will, to trust God and move forward in victory. With each new step,

Gideon's fear becomes weaker while his faith becomes stronger.

Identifying your fear and its "triggers" will help deprive those triggers of their power. Your regular, repeated exposure to a trigger (something that initiates a sense of fear or danger) can help to desensitize you to it. If your fear is situational or if you are under medical care for panic attacks, you can move toward victory as you walk through the following process:

> **"Prepare your minds for action;**
> **be self-controlled."**
> **(1 Peter 1:13)**

Moving from Panic to Peace

If you are overly sensitive to an object or situation, "desensitization" can be the key to open the door to freedom. Systematically repeat each of the following steps one at a time. After repeating one individual step day after day for a week or two, or until you no longer have a strong emotional reaction, move on to the next step. A slight reaction is expected and permissible before moving to the next step.

▶**Gradually increase your exposure to the fear.**

Specific Phobia—*Example: fear of elevators*

- Stand near an elevator and watch people get on and off.

- Push the button *as if* you are getting ready to step inside.

- Step inside (when other people are not around), hold the "Door Open" button, count to five and step out.

- Step inside, (again, when others are not around), hold the "Door Open" button, count to ten and step out.

- Step inside, ride to only one floor and exit.

- Ride to two floors … three … eventually all the way up and down for ten minutes.

A supportive person can be present for each step—initially also doing the activity—then later not participating, but being present to encourage and praise.

▶**Practice facing your fear.**

Social Phobia—*Example: fear of initiating conversation*

- Initiate by simply saying "hello" with a smile.

- Practice being genuinely interested in each person you speak with. Think: *What is truly meaningful to this person?*—then mention it or ask about it.

- Listen carefully to what is said by others.

- Ask follow-up questions.

- Ask simple, open-ended questions of others about themselves—questions that can't be answered with just a "yes" or "no."

- Intentionally use "you" and "yours" more in conversations than you use "I" and "my."

- Make brief comments about yourself.

- Practice by asking a salesperson questions.

- Every day practice saying general questions you could ask anyone:

  — "Who has been the most influential person in your life?"

  — "What was your favorite subject in school?"

  — "What do you enjoy doing more than anything else?"

  — "What has brought you the greatest satisfaction in anything that you have done?"

▶ **Repeat each step over and over again until it evokes little reaction.**

Agoraphobia—*Example: fear of a panic attack (fear in open spaces)*

- Open your front door and leave it open.
- Stand in the open door for as long as possible.
- Go out the door and stand on the porch—breathe deeply.
- Walk down the sidewalk to the edge of your property.
- Walk around the outside of the house.
- Sit in the car while it is in the driveway.
- Have someone drive you around the block.
- Drive yourself around the block.
- Go to the mall and sit in your car in the parking lot.
- Go to the mall when it will not be too crowded and walk around.
- Go into a store and greet a sales clerk.
- Make a small purchase.

Each step of the way, say,

"The LORD is with me; I will not be afraid." (Psalm 118:6)

"Be strong and courageous. Do not be afraid or terrified because of them, for the LORD your God goes with you; he will never leave you nor forsake you." (Deuteronomy 31:6)

Note: For serious phobic reactions, the process of desensitization is almost always used in combination with professional medical help.

HOW TO Counter Your Fears with Facts

Like Gideon, if you grew up in an environment where fear reigned, you could easily have developed a fear-based mentality as a child and then grown into an adult who is now controlled by the fear. At times, you feel helpless and powerless to confront or to match someone strength-for-strength. Gideon had been at the mercy of those around him who, as "master manipulators," had a whole arsenal of fear tactics. Unless you, like Gideon, come to recognize the bondage you are in and accept the fact that Christ came to free the oppressed, you will remain in bondage. Yes, Christ came to set you free—just as He set Gideon free centuries before.

"The Spirit of the Lord is on me, because he has anointed me to preach good news to the poor. He has sent me to proclaim freedom for the prisoners and recovery of sight for the blind, to release the oppressed."
(Luke 4:18)

▶ **Fear:** "I can't help this feeling of intense fear!"

Fact: "This feeling is a bluff to my mind and body. It is not grounded in truth."

"Though an army besiege me, my heart will not fear; though war break out against me, even then will I be confident." (Psalm 27:3)

▶ **Fear:** "I have this feeling of doom—a feeling that I am going to die."

Fact: "The time of death is in God's hands. I will choose to trust Him."

"Man's days are determined; you have decreed the number of his months and have set limits he cannot exceed." (Job 14:5)

▶ **Fear:** "I'm afraid of what others are thinking about me."

Fact: "My peace comes from pleasing God, not in pleasing man."

"We make it our goal to please him."
(2 Corinthians 5:9)

▶**Fear:** "I am hopeless and can never change."

Fact: "In Christ, I am a new person. Nothing is hopeless."

"If anyone is in Christ, he is a new creation; the old has gone, the new has come!"
(2 Corinthians 5:17)

▶**Fear:** "I am so nervous, I can't think clearly."

Fact: "God will guard my mind and give me peace."

"The peace of God, which transcends all understanding, will guard your hearts and your minds in Christ Jesus."
(Philippians 4:7)

▶**Fear:** "To be safe, I have to be in control."

Fact: "God is in control of my life, and He is with me step-by-step."

"The LORD himself goes before you and will be with you; he will never leave you nor forsake you. Do not be afraid; do not be discouraged." (Deuteronomy 31:8)

▶**Fear:** "I feel trapped with no way of escape."

Fact: "God always makes a way of escape."

"No temptation has seized you except what is common to man. And God is faithful; he will not let you be tempted beyond what you can bear. But when you are tempted, he will also provide a way out so that you can stand up under it." (1 Corinthians 10:13)

QUESTION: "I want to conquer my fears. What do I need to do first?"

ANSWER: In reality, God is actually the One who does what He calls Gideon to do because *He is the One who enables Gideon to do it.* All God requires is that Gideon refuses to focus on the fear he feels and chooses to step forward in the faith he possesses. Of course, Gideon's faith increases as he faces each new fear-producing situation. He goes from fearfully tearing down his father's altar and Asherah pole under the cover of darkness to boldly pursuing the Midianites in the bright light of day!

"The one who calls you is faithful and he will do it." (1 Thessalonians 5:24)

Certain general things to consider when dealing with fears are often overlooked just because they are quite simple and too "obvious" to be seen. It's like looking at the forest but missing the trees. These suggestions may seem simplistic, but they can be the foundation on which to build an effective plan for overcoming unwanted fear and anxiety.

"He is like a man building a house, who dug down deep and laid the foundation on rock. When a flood came, the torrent struck that house but could not shake it, because it was well built." (Luke 6:48)

▶ Get a thorough medical check-up—ask if any condition could be causing anxiety.

▶ Ask your doctor to evaluate all medications.

▶ Get adequate sleep.

▶ Get regular exercise.

▶ Plan to get sufficient laughter, fun, and recreation.

▶ Be around encouraging people—remove yourself from negative people.

▶ Get on a healthy diet by eating healthful foods—avoid alcohol and drugs.

▶ Develop the habit of living one day at a time.

▶ Listen to inspirational Christian and/or classical music.

▶ Ask a trusted friend to help you; then imagine the worst and consider why it wouldn't be so bad after all.

"To him who is able to do immeasurably more than all we ask or imagine, according to his power that is at work within us."
(Ephesians 3:20)

DO'S AND DON'TS for Family and Friends[18]

Gideon does exactly what God requires. In time, he refuses to focus on his fear and chooses to step forward in faith. He knows he is not a mighty warrior, but he learns that God can be the warrior within him! It's not complicated—his supernatural victory comes simply because Gideon walks both fearfully with God by faith and fearlessly with God by faith.

Sometimes God chooses a specific person—friend or family member—to walk with the one who needs more faith. Just as God told Gideon to take Purah with him into the Midianite camp, fearful people need fearless friends to walk alongside to help them find the road to freedom.

▶ Those who are fearful need a friend.

▶ Those who are timid need a teammate.

▶ Those who are worried need someone wise.

▶ Those who are anxious need an exhorter.

▶ Those who cower need an encourager.

▶ Those who are tormented by fear need inspiration from those who have found freedom from fear.

To support a loved one who is struggling with fear, learn what to do and what not to do. You can very well be that person's answer to prayer.

**"There is a friend who sticks closer than a brother."
(Proverbs 18:24)**

▶ **Don't** become impatient when you don't understand their fear.

Do understand that what fearful people *feel* is *real*.

"A patient man has great understanding, but a quick-tempered man displays folly." (Proverbs 14:29)

▶ **Don't** think they are doing this for attention.

Do realize they are embarrassed and want to change.

"I do not understand what I do. For what I want to do I do not do, but what I hate I do." (Romans 7:15)

▶**Don't** be critical or use demeaning statements.

Do be gentle and supportive, and build up their self-confidence.

"Encourage one another and build each other up, just as in fact you are doing." (1 Thessalonians 5:11)

▶**Don't** assume you know what is best.

Do ask how you can help.

"We urge you, brothers, warn those who are idle, encourage the timid, help the weak, be patient with everyone." (1 Thessalonians 5:14)

▶**Don't** make them face a threatening situation without planning.

Do give them instruction in positive self-talk and relaxation exercises.

"Hold on to instruction, do not let it go; guard it well, for it is your life." (Proverbs 4:13)

▶**Don't** make them face the situation alone.

Do be there and assure them of your support.

"Two are better than one, because they have a good return for their work: If one falls

down, his friend can help him up. But pity the man who falls and has no one to help him up!" (Ecclesiastes 4:9–10)

▶ **Don't** begin with difficult situations.

Do help them to begin facing their fear in small increments.

"Consider it pure joy, my brothers, whenever you face trials of many kinds, because you know that the testing of your faith develops perseverance." (James 1:2–3)

▶ **Don't** constantly ask, "How are you feeling?"

Do help them see the value of having other interests.

"Each of you should look not only to your own interests, but also to the interests of others." (Philippians 2:4)

▶ **Don't** show disappointment and displeasure if they fail.

Do encourage them and compliment their efforts to conquer their fear.

"Do not withhold good from those who deserve it, when it is in your power to act." (Proverbs 3:27)

▶**Don't** *say,* "Don't be absurd; there's nothing for you to fear!"

Do *say,* "No matter how you feel, tell yourself the truth, 'I will take one step at a time.'"

"The wise in heart are called discerning, and pleasant words promote instruction." (Proverbs 16:21)

▶**Don't** *say,* "Don't be a coward; you have to do this!"

Do *say,* "I know this is difficult for you, but it's not dangerous. You have the courage to do this."

"A wise man's heart guides his mouth, and his lips promote instruction." (Proverbs 16:23)

▶**Don't** *say,* "Quit living in the past; this is not that bad."

Do *say,* "Remember to stay in the present and remind yourself, 'That was then, and this is now.'"

"Pleasant words are a honeycomb, sweet to the soul and healing to the bones." (Proverbs 16:24)

Epilogue

Among the thousands and thousands of people mentioned in the Bible, Gideon is selected by God to be one of the few in His famous "Hall of Faith." Hebrews chapter 11, commonly called "The Hall of Faith," illustrates the power of living by faith and extols the predominant *heroes of the faith*. Fewer than twenty names are listed on this *Honor Roll of Old Testament Saints*. Gideon is one of the rare few: *"Gideon … who through faith conquered kingdoms, administered justice, and gained what was promised"* (Hebrews 11:32–33).

His transformation from being fearfully timid to being *fearlessly triumphant* is evident as he confronts the captive kings of Midian. Asking what kind of men they had killed at Tabor, Gideon's once fearsome enemies reply, *"'Men like you,' they answered, 'each one with the bearing of a prince'"* (Judges 8:18).

Instead of retreating in fear, the once meek man from the small clan of Manasseh now bears a princely posture and has become a powerful warrior—the *"mighty warrior"* God called him to be.

SCRIPTURES TO MEMORIZE

When will the Lord **deliver me from all my fears?**

> *"I sought the LORD, and he answered me; **he delivered me from all my fears**."* (Psalm 34:4)

What should you **set your mind on** when you're afraid?

> *"**Set your minds on** things above, not on earthly things. For you died, and your life is now hidden with Christ in God."* (Colossians 3:2–3)

Why am I to **cast all my anxiety on Him?**

> *"Humble yourselves, therefore, under God's mighty hand, that he may lift you up in due time. **Cast all your anxiety on him** because he cares for you."* (1 Peter 5:6–7)

Why does the Bible ask **of whom shall I be afraid?**

> *"The LORD is my light and my salvation—whom shall I fear? The LORD is the stronghold of my life—**of whom shall I be afraid?**"* (Psalm 27:1)

Why should I **not be afraid and not be discouraged?**

> *"The LORD himself goes before you and will be with you; he will never leave you nor forsake you. **Do not be afraid; do not be discouraged**."* (Deuteronomy 31:8)

What will happen when **God is our refuge**?

*"**God is our refuge** and strength, an ever-present help in trouble."* (Psalm 46:1)

How can you **guard your heart and your mind** when you have no **peace**?

*"The **peace** of God, which transcends all understanding, will **guard your hearts and your minds** in Christ Jesus."* (Philippians 4:7)

Why does the Lord say **do not fear** and **do not be dismayed**?

*"**Do not fear**, for I am with you; **do not be dismayed**, for I am your God. I will strengthen you and help you; I will uphold you with my righteous right hand."* (Isaiah 41:10)

Why is **there no fear in love**?

*"**There is no fear in love**. But perfect love drives out fear, because fear has to do with punishment. The one who fears is not made perfect in love."* (1 John 4:18)

What will happen if **the Lord is my shepherd**?

*"**The LORD is my shepherd**, I shall not be in want. He makes me lie down in green pastures, he leads me beside quiet waters, he restores my soul. He guides me in paths of righteousness for his name's sake. Even though I walk through the valley of the shadow of death, I will fear no evil, for you are with me; your rod and your staff, they comfort me."* (Psalm 23:1–4)

NOTES

1. *American Heritage Electronic Dictionary* (Houghton Mifflin, 1992), s.v. "To Fear."

2. W.E. Vine, Merrill F. Unger, and William White, *Vine's Expository Dictionary of Biblical Words* (New York: Thomas Nelson, 1985), s.v. "Fear."

3. Lawrence O. Richards, *The Bible Readers' Companion* (Wheaton, IL: Victor Books, 1991), 72.

4. Mary Lynn Hendrix, *Understanding Panic Disorders* (US Department of Health and Human Service, National Institute of Health), 2.

5. Mary Lynn Hendrix, *Understanding Panic Disorders*, 2–3.

6. *New Oxford Dictionary of English*, electronic ed., (Oxford University Press, 1998), s.v. "Phobia."

7. Vine, Unger, and White, *Vine's Complete Expository Dictionary of Biblical Words*, electronic ed., s.v. "Fear, Fearful, Fearfulness."

8. Vine, Unger, and White, *Vine's Complete Expository Dictionary of Biblical Words*, electronic ed., s.v. "Fear, Fearful, Fearfulness."

9. Oaklawn Toward Health and Wholeness, *What Everyone Should Know About Anxiety Disorders* (South Deerfield, MA: Channing L. Bete, Co., 1994), 2–3.

10. Kevin R. Kracke, "Phobic Disorders," *Baker Encyclopedia of Psychology & Counseling*, 2nd ed., ed. David G. Benner and Peter C. Hill

(Grand Rapids: Baker, 1999), 871–872.

11. For this section, see Kracke, "Phobic Disorders," *Baker Encyclopedia of Psychology & Counseling*, 2nd ed., 871–8. Kracke renames the simple phobia as specific phobia.

12. American Psychiatric Association, *Diagnostic and Statistical Manual of Mental Disorders: DSM-III-R.* 3rd ed. (Washington, DC: American Psychiatric Association, 1987), 432.

13. Phobia Center of the Southwest, "Agoraphobia," 1990, n.d.

14. Karen Randau, *Conquering Fear* (Dallas: Rapha, 1991), 41–56.

15. Lawrence J. Crabb, Jr., *Understanding People: Deep Longings for Relationship*, Ministry Resources Library (Grand Rapids: Zondervan, 1987), 15–16; Robert S. McGee, *The Search for Significance*, 2nd ed. (Houston, TX: Rapha, 1990), 27–30.

16. Randau, *Conquering Fear*, 41–56.

17. Leslie Parrott, III, "Systematic Desensitization," *Baker Encyclopedia of Psychology & Counseling*, 2nd ed., ed. David G. Benner and Peter C. Hill (Grand Rapids: Baker, 1999), 1193.

18. Shirley Babior and Carol Goldman, *Overcoming Panic Attacks: Strategies to Free Yourself from the Anxiety Trap* (Minneapolis, MN: CompCare, 1990), 59–62.

SELECTED BIBLIOGRAPHY

Agoraphobia. Dallas: Phobia Center of the Southwest, 1990.

American Psychiatric Association. *Diagnostic and Statistical Manual of Mental Disorders: DSM-III-R*. 3rd ed. Washington, DC: American Psychiatric Association, 1987.

Babior, Shirley, and Carol Goldman. *Overcoming Panic Attacks: Strategies to Free Yourself from the Anxiety Trap*. Minneapolis, MN: CompCare, 1990.

Carothers, Merlin R. *From Fear to Faith*. Nashville: Thomas Nelson, 1997.

Crabb, Lawrence J., Jr. *Understanding People: Deep Longings for Relationship*. Ministry Resources Library. Grand Rapids: Zondervan, 1987.

Dolph, Charles D. "Panic Attack." *Baker Encyclopedia of Psychology & Counseling*, 2nd ed., edited by David G. Benner and Peter C. Hill, 818–19. Grand Rapids: Baker, 1999.

Hunt, June. *Counseling Through Your Bible Handbook*. Eugene, Oregon: Harvest House Publishers, 2008.

Hunt, June. *How to Forgive . . . When You Don't Feel Like It*. Eugene, Oregon: Harvest House Publishers, 2007.

Hunt, June. *Seeing Yourself Through God's Eyes*. Eugene, Oregon: Harvest House Publishers 2008.

Ingrid, Gary. *Hearts of Iron, Feet of Clay.* Chicago: Moody, 1979.

Kracke, Kevin R. "Phobic Disorders." *Baker Encyclopedia of Psychology & Counseling*, 2nd ed, edited by David G. Benner and Peter C. Hill, 871–72. Grand Rapids: Baker, 1999.

Larson, David E., editor, *Mayo Clinic Family Health Book.* New York: W. Morrow, 1990.

McGee, Robert S. *The Search for Significance.* 2nd ed. Houston, TX: Rapha, 1990.

Meier, Paul D., Frank B. Minirth, and Frank B. Wichern. *Introduction to Psychology and Counseling: Christian Perspectives and Applications.* Grand Rapids: Baker, 1982.

Parrott, Leslie, III. "Systematic Desensitization." *Baker Encyclopedia of Psychology & Counseling*, 2nd ed, edited by David G. Benner and Peter C. Hill, 1193. Grand Rapids: Baker, 1999.

Randau, Karen. *Anxiety Attacks.* Dallas: Rapha, 1991.

Randau, Karen. *Conquering Fear.* Dallas: Rapha, 1991.

Wright, H. Norman. *Afraid No More!* Wheaton, IL: Tyndale House, 1992.

HOPE FOR THE HEART TITLES

Adultery ....ISBN 9781596366848
Alcohol & Drug Abuse...ISBN 9781596366596
Anger ....ISBN 9781596366411
Anorexia & Bulimia .... ISBN 9781596369313
Bullying ....ISBN 9781596369269
Chronic Illness & Disability...............................ISBN 9781628621464
Codependency ....ISBN 9781596366510
Conflict Resolution ....ISBN 9781596366473
Confrontation...ISBN 9781596366886
Considering Marriage .... ISBN 9781596366763
Critical Spirit.. ISBN 9781628621310
Decision Making ....ISBN 9781596366534
Depression..ISBN 9781596366497
Domestic Violence..ISBN 9781596366824
Dysfunctional Family ....ISBN 9781596369368
Fear ....ISBN 9781596366701
Financial Freedom .... ISBN 9781596369412
Forgiveness...ISBN 9781596366435
Friendship ....ISBN 9781596368828
Gambling ....ISBN 9781596366862
Grief ....ISBN 9781596366572
Guilt ....ISBN 9781596366961
Hope ....ISBN 9781596366558
Loneliness ....ISBN 9781596366909
Manipulation... ISBN 9781596366749
Marriage.. ISBN 9781596368941
Overeating..ISBN 9781596369467
Parenting ....ISBN 9781596366725
Perfectionism... ISBN 9781596369214
Procrastination ....ISBN 9781628621648
Reconciliation..ISBN 9781596368897
Rejection ....ISBN 9781596366787
Self-Worth..ISBN 9781596366688
Sexual Integrity ....ISBN 9781596366947
Singleness .... ISBN 9781596368774
Spiritual Abuse .... ISBN 9781628621266
Stress ....ISBN 9781596368996
Success Through Failure ....ISBN 9781596366923
Suicide Prevention...ISBN 9781596366800
Trials .... ISBN 9781628621891
Verbal & Emotional Abuse ....ISBN 9781596366459
Victimization..ISBN 9781628621365

www.aspirepress.com

The HOPE FOR THE HEART Biblical Counseling Library is Your Solution!

- Easy-to-read, perfect for anyone.
- Short. Only 96 pages. Good for the busy person.
- Christ-centered biblical advice and practical help
- Tested and proven over 20 years of June Hunt's radio ministry
- 30 titles in the series – each tackling a key issue people face today.
- Affordable. You or your church can give away, lend, or sell them.

Display available for churches and ministries.

www.aspirepress.com